THE

MYSTIC COAST

STONINGTON TO NEW LONDON

A PHOTOGRAPHIC PORTRAIT

• PILOTPRESS PUBLISHERS •
TWIN LIGHTS PUBLISHERS

First published in the United States of America by
PilotPress Publishers, Inc.
James R. Franklin, Publisher
110 Westchester Road
Newton, Massachusetts 02458
Telephone: (617) 332-0703
http://www.PilotPress.com

and

Twin Lights Publishers, Inc.
Doris R. Patey, Publisher
10 Hale Street
Rockport, Massachusetts 01966
Telephone: (978) 546-7398
http://www.twinlightspub.com

ISBN 1-885435-09-6

10 9 8 7 6 5 4 3 2 1

Book design by
SYP Design & Production
http://www.sypdesign.com

Cover image: Stephen Sisk

Printed in China

CONTENTS

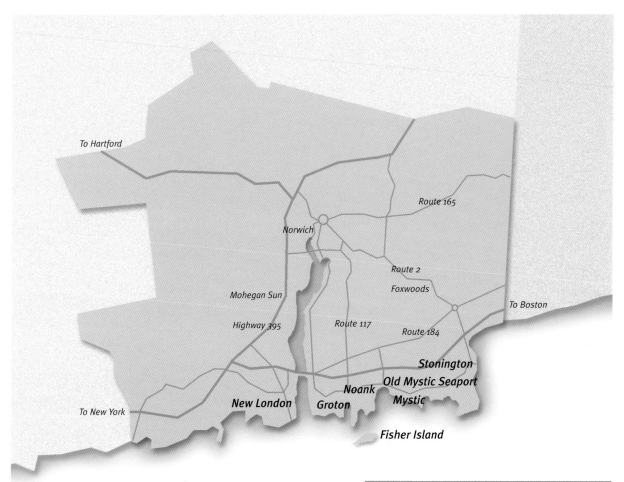

To Hartford

Route 165

Norwich

Route 2

Mohegan Sun

Foxwoods

To Boston

Highway 395

Route 117

Route 184

Stonington

Old Mystic Seaport

Noank

Mystic

New London

Groton

To New York

Fisher Island

The region selected for this book is comprised of several towns whose history is coincident with the history of Connecticut; its association with the sea and a ship building tradition dating back to the 1650s. While each town is uniquely independent and has a beauty all its own, all of the towns along the coast, as well as those a bit inland, add to the character of Mystic and the Mystic Coast

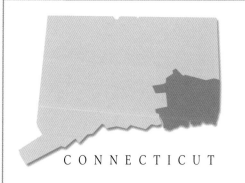

CONNECTICUT

ACKNOWLEDGEMENTS

The publishers would like to acknowledge many people who helped with this book.

The Mystic Color Lab assisted us with the contest as well as the judging. Special thanks are offered to Edward McCabe, President, Colleen Garringer, Director of Marketing, Carrie Glas, Product Manager, Sandy Onorato, Marketing Production Manager and Cally Haserot, Acquisition Manager. Visit their website at www.mysticcolorlab.com.

The Mystic Chamber of Commerce for their valuable advice. Visit their website at www.mysticchamber.org.

Thanks go to Michael Costanza for creating the provocative captions. A life-long resident of Stonington, his knowledge of the area significantly expanded upon the images.

Brenda Swithenbank's continued suggestions, support and encouragement is always invaluable.

FOREWORD

PilotPress Publishers and Twin Lights Publishers are pleased to bring you this photographic portrait.

The book presents many quality photographs of the Mystic area that is the work of amateur, semi-professional and professional photographers who submitted their work as part of a photographic contest.

These photographs are representative of the area. We ask that you view them with the same enthusiasm and excitement experienced by the photographers who live in or who visited the area and were prompted to record their memories on film.

We would like to congratulate all whose work was selected for this book and, in particular, the first, second, and third prize winners highlighted on the following pages.

First Prize
Stonington Village at Sunrise
Stephen Sisk, Stonington, CT

Stephen Sisk is a life long resident of Stonington. His inspiration comes from his passion for the outdoors. He enjoys the creative aspects of photographing the Mystic coastal region, and has found the Mystic coastal region to offer a wealth of photographic subjects and settings throughout the year. A self-taught photographer, Steve has been photographing the local area for over twenty years.

Second Prize
Mystic Waterfront
John Williams, Rockport, MA

John Williams grew up on Greater Boston's North Shore, and was fascinated by photography at an early age. At 14 he had his own darkroom and he studied at the New York Institute of Photography.

Boats and seascapes are his favorite subjects. He and his wife have traveled and photographed from picturesque Nova Scotia to Oregon, and throughout New England and eastern Massachusetts where they now reside.

Recently, while visiting relatives, he fell in love with Mystic and plans to return again and again.

Third Prize
West side of Stonington
Borough facing harbor
Thomas Carver, Stonington, CT

Thomas Carver spent his childhood years growing up in Stonington Borough that in the 1960's was a working class town. A Christmas gift of a Kodak Instamatic camera began a photographic journey that continues today.

Captivated by the Pacific Northwest's fabulous scenery while attending college in the Seattle area, a job as a newspaper photographer after graduation turned hobby into profession. After ten years in the Northwest, a move to California to attend the Brooks Institute of Photography resulted in an editorial position for a highly photo-oriented magazine.

Returning to Stonington in 1990, Mr. Carver documents those aspects of New England's flavor that is our heritage, a simpler and slower lifestyle ruled by the land, the sea, and the four seasons.

Mr. Carver is a partner/owner of the Harvest Moon Market & Deli in downtown Mystic as well as a railroad locomotive leasing business.

STONINGTON

Sailboats speckle Stonington Harbor. The only open-ocean port along the Connecticut coast, which is otherwise guarded by Long Island, the harbor made a convenient base for rumrunners during Prohibition. As village resident Henry Robinson Palmer wrote, even when Coast Guard ships frightened some of the rumrunners into dumping their cargoes overboard, "such caches became fair prey for certain local residents" brave enough to fish them out.

The Pawcatuck River winds its way between the rural, seaside towns of Stonington, Connecticut, and Westerly, Rhode Island. Hundreds of years ago, the river formed a rough territorial boundary between the Pequot and the Narragansett American Indian tribes. Years later, the European settlers of Connecticut, Rhode Island, and Massachusetts would dispute each other's land claims near the river.

3

1

The sails of a fleet of dinghies create a colorful collage on the Mystic River. Recreational and competitive boaters sail up and down the tidal estuary at all times of the year.

Bryce Breen
Canon Rebel EOS,
Kodak 200 35mm

2

A sailboat plays off aptly named Sandy Point, the northern tip of a narrow sandbar in Little Narragansett Bay, just off Stonington. Most of the island lies within Rhode Island waters. In fact, the sandbar was connected to nearby Watch Hill, Rhode Island, until the great Hurricane of 1938 ripped through southern New England.

John Williams
Nikon 6006, 28 - 80 zoom,
Fujicolor 200 f/16, 1/250

3

A late-winter snow has dusted the fields of this farm in North Stonington. Incorporated in 1807 from Stonington, the rural town offers a collection of delightful sights to those visitors willing to stray from the beaten path, including several working dairy farms, acres of state forest, and miles of country roads lined with stone walls. The town also claims to have more cemeteries than any other town in the country. One gravestone on Hangman Hill Road marks the final resting place of a former resident's favorite horse.

Stephen Sisk
Nikon 8008, Tamron 28-200
zoom, Fujichrome Velvia, f/11

3

1

The vibrant colors of fall, a handsome barn, and an ageless stonewall—Stonington at its best, along the old Pequot Trail. Established as the town's first road in 1669, the trail ran from the head of the Mystic River in modern-day Old Mystic to Kichemaug, now known as Westerly, Rhode Island. In 1990 Pequot Trail became the first road in Connecticut to receive scenic status and protection.

Stephen Sisk
Nikon 8008, Sigma 18-32mm
zoom, Fujichrome Velvia, f/22

2

A battered barn on Taugwonk Road. Part of the town's so-called uplands, the scenic road is home to old farms and to the renowned Stonington Vineyards, where visitors can enjoy wine tastings and winery tours.

Rowena Melville-Young

3

The setting sun peaks out from under the pavilion at du Bois Beach on Stonington Point. The beach is named for the late Coert du Bois, who spearheaded its creation in 1956 while he was the president of the Village Improvement Association.

Stephen Sisk
Nikon 8008, Tamron 28-200
zoom, Fujichrome Velvia, f/5.6

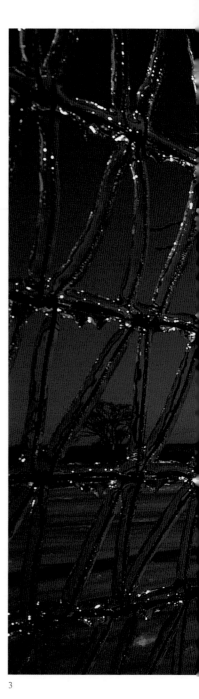

1

2

3

(previous page)

Dock pilings at Dodson's Boat Yard stand at attention to admire a commanding sunset on Stonington Harbor.

Stephen Sisk
Nikon 8008, Sigma 18-32mm
zoom, Fujichrome Velvia, f/2.8

1

A white Christmas at the First Congregational Church of Stonington, better known as the Road Church. Founded in 1674 along the town's only road at the time, the Pequot Trail, the church is the oldest in Stonington and the seventh oldest in Connecticut. Its main doors are located behind the chancel, so that churchgoers enter next to the pulpit and must face the entire congregation if they arrive late for worship.

Stephen Sisk
Nikon 8008, Sigma 18-32mm
zoom, Fujichrome Velvia

2

At Cannon Square in Stonington Borough stand the very guns with which village residents fended off five British warships in August 1814. Despite heavy fire from the attackers' own cannons, the village lost not a single life or home. Cannon balls left behind are displayed today at the Old Lighthouse Museum at the end of Water Street. The borough's Warden and Burgesses erected a granite marker at Stonington Point in 1956 to commemorate the battle. Borough residents to this day commonly describe the location of their homes as north or south "of the cannons."

Thomas Carver
Pentax 6x7, PK-64 Roll Film

3

Shimmering or shivering? A fence at the Manatuck Farm in Stonington waits for the sun to melt away the icy coating left behind by a recent storm.

Thomas Carver
Nikon FM-2, Kodachrome 25,
f/5.6 1/250

1
2

3

1

The rays of the sun climb the winding granite stairwell of the Stonington light.

Richard D. Dixon

2

Peering into the second floor of the Old Lighthouse Museum from the light tower's staircase. The museum contains countless relics from Stonington's sealing and whaling ships, as well as displays on other local lighthouses.

Richard D. Dixon

3

The Stonington light was moved a short distance inland in 1840 as storms threatened to wash away the tip of Stonington Point. Many of the original granite stones were used in rebuilding the octagonal tower, to which a new keeper's house was attached. A sixth-order Fresnel lens was installed in the tower in 1856 and remained in use until 1889, when a new beacon was built on the harbor's outer breakwater. The lens sits today inside the museum.

John Williams
Nikon 6006, Kodak
Gold 100 f/11, 1/250

1

1

Above a fireplace at the Old Lighthouse Museum, a portrait of David Chesebrough, great-grandson of Stonington's first white settler, flirts with the idea of smiling. William Chesebrough established the town's first settlement at Wequetequock Cove in 1649. Chesebrough had arrived in America years before with John Winthrop, whose company settled Boston in 1630 and whose son would settle Groton, Connecticut. Along with Thomas Stanton, Thomas Miner, and Walter Palmer, Chesebrough is considered one of Stonington's four founders.

Beth Mulloy
Nikon N70 ASA 100

2

The Old Lighthouse Museum on Stonington Point. Built in 1823, it is the oldest government lighthouse in Connecticut. Three states are visible from its 30-foot stone tower, which once supported a lantern with ten oil lamps and silver reflectors. Home to a Stonington Historical Society museum since 1927, the lighthouse served as a beacon to the whaling ships and fishing vessels that made Stonington Harbor one of the region's busiest during the 19th century.

Marilyn Cruthers
Nikon F6, Mystic
Color Lab film 200

2

1

1

Built in 1900, North Stonington's
Wheeler Library also served for years as
the town's school. The modern-day
Wheeler High School, located just next
door, takes its mascot—the Lion—from
the twin lion sculptures that guard the
library's steps. The library's upstairs win-
dows offer a commanding view of North
Stonington's quiet village, formerly
known as Milltown. The village contains
several colonial-era homes, the town
green, a Congregational and a Baptist
church, the Town Hall, a hardware store,
and an old grist mill with a water wheel
on Shunock Brook.

Rowena Melville-Young

2

Architectural gems from the village's
seafaring days, the 18th- and 19th-centu-
ry homes of sea captains and proud
patriots line the streets of Stonington
Borough. Among the homes along Water
Street can be found the birthplace of
Capt. Nathaniel B. Palmer, who discovered the continent of Antarctica in 1820
while commanding the sloop Hero on a
sealing trip. Only 21 at the time, Palmer
recorded in his log finding "land not yet
laid down on my chart." The Stonington
Historical Society maintains a museum
in his adult home, a 16-room mansion
on Palmer Street.

John Williams
Nikon 6006, Kodak
Gold 100 f/8, 1/250

2

1

2

1

One of the area's better looking sun-worshippers catches some rays on Lord's Point. Visitors to Stonington can find seals in the waters of Fishers Island Sound or at the more convenient location of Mystic Aquarium, Connecticut's most popular tourist attraction.

Marion Krepcio
Pentax Asa 200, f/125

2

Rowboats rest peacefully in quiet Quiambaug Cove, beside the Miner Burial Ground, one of Stonington's many cemeteries. The Stonington Historical Society counts 61 graveyards in town, and several more remote family burial sites dot the countryside. Some graves date back to the 17th century.

Laura Kahler
Canon AE1, Mystic
Color Lab 200

1

1

Crammed into their berths at the Town Dock, several of the Stonington fishing fleet's ships wait for their next trip to sea. Many ships find their catch in Georges Bank, the submerged sandbank east of Massachusetts.

Laura Kahler
Canon AE1, Mystic
Color Lab 200, f/11

2

Diesel-powered draggers and tangle of nets bask in the warmth of an August afternoon in Stonington Harbor, home to Connecticut's last commercial fishing fleet. The fleet's two dozen ships harvest a variety of species in the waters off New England, from flounder and lobster to scallops and squid. Fishermen must battle more than the sea, however. Government catch quotas, rising insurance costs, and volatile markets make their profession a particularly challenging one. The Stonington fleet has petitioned—and even sued—the federal government in recent years to change its quotas for summer flounder.

Viola Breit
Olympus Stylus zoom DLX automatic,
Mystic Color Print 35mm 200

2

2

1

Balloons dance in the breeze at Stonington's annual Blessing of the Fleet, a festival meant for celebrating generations of the community's Portuguese fishing families—and for remembering those fishermen lost at sea. Thousands attend each summer, devouring lobsters, clam chowder, and Portuguese cuisine and dancing late into the night at the Town Dock. The actual blessing comes when a wreath is tossed from a boat into the waters beyond the harbor breakwater, with Roman Catholic clergy on hand.

Margaret L. Pratt
Canon A2 - Auto

2

Friends and family and other revelers celebrate on board Robin Guzzo's dragger *Jenna Lynn* during the Blessing Boat Parade. The fear of lawsuits has made some fishermen less willing to invite strangers aboard in recent years, however.

Margaret L. Pratt
Canon A2 - Auto

1

This sunset at Stonington Point lights
the harbor on fire.

Carol Cattanach
Kodak Advantik 1600
Auto, 200 speed

2

A sailboat at its mooring in Stonington
Harbor bids farewell to the sun as its
sets over Wamphassuc Point.

Elizabeth Hall

MYSTIC, OLD MYSTIC, AND MYSTIC SEAPORT

The name Mystic is derived from the Pequot Indian name "missi-tuk" which means "great tidal river" as the Mystic River is really an estuary, and it's waters advance and retreat with the tides.

Historic homes, church steeples, and countless shops, ships, and marinas dot the shores of the river through downtown Mystic. The railroad swing bridge remains open for boats to sail in and out of the village, and closes for trains on their way to New York or Boston.

Founded on Christmas day in 1929, The Mystic Seaport Museum has grown into perhaps the world's premier maritime museum.

2

3

1
The Seaport Light. This sparkplug light is a reproduction of New England's second oldest lighthouse—Nantucket's Brant Point Light, which was built in 1746. At only 26 feet, the two lights are the shortest in New England. Both contain fourth-order Fresnel lenses.

Lynda Hodgins
Canon Rebel 2000 / EOS 300,
Kodak Max 400, f/22

2
New Haven sharpies like this 35-footer at Mystic Seaport tonged for oysters along the Connecticut shore. The boats could be rigged with one or two sails, and their maneuverability made them popular with shellfishermen up and down the Atlantic coast.

Lynda Hodgins
Canon Rebel 2000 / EOS 300,
Kodak Max 400, f/22

3
Wind ripples the Mystic River and the broad sail of the catboat Breck Marshall as it glides past the Seaport Light. The 20-foot wooden ship is a replica of the fishing cat boats used at the turn of the last century. At 392 square feet, the ship's sail is the largest of any boat that sails the Mystic River north of the drawbridge.

Bryce Breen
Canon Rebel EOS,
Kodak 200 35mm

1

The lavender hue of sunset melts into the Mystic River along a Masons Island dock.

Cheryl Kraynak
Ektachrome 200, f4, 1/15

2

Weathered old lobster pots at Mystic Seaport, traps for New England's tastiest seafood treat.

Stephen Sisk
Nikon 8008, Sigma 18-32mm
zoom, Fujichrome Velvia, f/16

2

1

2

(*previous page*)

Blue heaven: gazing north up the Mystic River.

Thomas Carver
Nikon FM-2, Nikkor 180 telephoto,
Fuji Velvia, f/5.6 1/250

3

1

The ships of the Mystic River wait for daybreak to chase away the haze of early morning. Mirror-like reflections on the still river offer a lesson in symmetry.

Peter Breit
Contax 167 MT,
Kodak Max T400, f/16

2

A ghostly evening fog drifts into downtown Mystic and settles down for the night beside the drawbridge. The salty seawater of the Mystic River, which is really a tidal estuary, retains the warmth of summer long after the cool air of autumn arrives in town, making misty nights a common sight.

Peter Breit
Contax 167 MT,
Kodak Max T400, f/16

3

Mystic Seaport's Regina M. teeters atop a reflection of itself in the glassy Mystic River. Built in Maine in 1900 as a sloop, the ship today mimics the style of the pinky schooners that fished the Grand Banks between 1820 and 1860.

Marilyn Cruthers
Nikon F6, Mystic
Color Lab film 200

1

1

Some of downtown Mystic's most coveted real estate: the Mystic River shimmers beneath the condominiums that line its west bank at Steamboat Wharf. The schooner Argia rests with its sails down outside the Steamboat Inn.

Betsy Hickey
Minolta Maxxum Htsi
Plus Automatic, Kodak 400

2

A Wednesday evening Beetle Cat race on the Mystic River. Mystic Seaport rents out the boats for weekly races during the summer and for a few Saturday races in the fall. The Beetle Cat has remained popular with sailors of all skill levels since John Beetle built the first in New Bedford, Massachusetts, in 1921.

Richard D. Dixon

2

3

1

The Mystic River Drawbridge makes way for the steamship Sabino, bound for Noank and Fishers Island Sound. The Sabino's captain and the bridge tender often toot their horns to each other as a friendly "hello.

Carol Cattanach
Kodak Advantix 1600 Auto,
200 speed

2

The boardwalk at the Mystic River Park, next to the drawbridge, offers the perfect setting for early morning reflections on the river.

John Williams
Nikon 6006,
Kodak Gold 100 f/11, 1/125

3

A boater races past the North Dumpling Light, just off Fishers Island. Built in 1849, the tower stands 31 feet tall and contains the most powerful light in Fishers Island Sound. Governor John Winthrop of the Massachusetts Bay Colony, the father of the founder of Groton, bought North Dumpling Island in 1639 from an American Indian tribe, and it remained in his family for more than two centuries.

John Williams
Nikon 6006, 28 - 80 zoom,
Fujicolor 200 F11, 1/250

1

2

1

Spectators pack the Mystic River Park each July for the Antique & Classic Boat Rendezvous, hosted by Mystic Seaport. The extra curious maritime enthusiasts paddle out for a closer look at their favorite vessels.

Viola Breit
Olympus Stylus zoom DLX automatic,
Mystic Color Print 35mm 200

2

Pigeons share a snack in the Mystic River Park. The galleries of the Mystic Art Association sit directly across the river. For the last four decades, the streets of downtown have played host to the Mystic Outdoor Art Festival, which attracts hundreds of artists and thousands of art lovers each August.

Betsy Hickey
Minolta Maxxum Htsi Plus
Automatic, Kodak 400

1

1

Looking west across the Mystic River, a tugboat docked at Mystic Seaport's shipyard seems to be admiring the old captains' homes along Gravel Street. The steeple of Union Baptist Church peeks out above the trees in downtown. These same hills were once home to the Pequot Indians, who dominated the region until Capt. John Mason and his native allies seized their fort in a brutal battle in 1637.

Marilyn Chittom
Advantix 3600, Fujicolor
Smart Film 200

2

A bright and buoyant blob, a tugboat heads downriver in Mystic.

Pam Reed
Minolta Maxxum 5000i,
Sigma 70-210mm zoom,
autofocus, asa400 35mm print

2

1

2

3

1

The Sandra-Michelle, a working fishing vessel, docked at the village of Noank. Located at the mouth of the Mystic River, Noank contains several marinas and boatyards.

John Williams
Nikon N70, Kodak
Gold 100 F11, 1/125

2

Mystic Seaport's Sabino has carried more than a million visitors up and down the Mystic River since 1973. Built in 1908 in East Boothbay, Maine, the ship was christened Tourist. Ironically, its first engine was made in Noank. Tourist sank on the Damariscotta River in Maine in 1918, but was raised and renamed Sabino, after Sabino Hill on the Kennebec River. Visitors often mispronounce its name, which, by the way, contains a long *I*. Today, the Sa-bye-no is the last coal-powered, wooden steam ferry in the country.

John Williams
Nikon N70, Kodak
Gold 100 F8, 1/250

3

Schooners congregate near the Morgan, as seen from the Conrad just downstream.

Joel Peterson

1

2

3

1

The Mystic River Drawbridge on U.S. Route 1 opens thousands of times each year to let boats pass through downtown, and thousands of motorists drive across its deck at the Groton/Stonington border. During the summer, the bridge opens hourly at quarter past the hour. The resulting traffic delays produce different results in different people. Vacationers often pause to photograph the bridge, while many locals head for their favorite shortcuts. Built in 1922, the drawbridge is the oldest bascule bridge in the country. It is undoubtedly Mystic's most famous landmark.

Michael Marusic
Minolta X6-Asoligor 80-200mm
Zoom F5.6, Kodak Gold 200

2

Mystic Seaport's preservation shipyard and the steam ferry Sabino, as spied from between the spokes of one of the wheels that lifts the Mystic River Drawbridge. The bascule bridge uses two motors and two giant wheels to lift its counterweights.

Mary S. Georgetti
Pentax SF1, Kodak film

3

The schooner Argia docks permanently at Steamboat Wharf in downtown Mystic, next to the drawbridge. Visitors can sail on the Argia into Fishers Island Sound for sunset tours, and local students often study the marine life of the Mystic River during field trips on board.

John Williams
Nikon N70, Kodak
Gold 100 F8, 1/250

1
2

1

These tiny boats aspire to greater things as they learn to sail in the shadow of the whaler *Charles W. Morgan*.

Jeff Feldmann
Sensia 100, N90S,
Sigma 400

2

A family of osprey enjoys its bird's-eye view high above the Mystic River.

Jeff Feldmann
Sensia 100, N90S,
f4.8, Sigma 400

3

The training ship Joseph Conrad was launched in Copenhagen, Denmark, in 1882. The iron-hulled ship was named then the Georg Stage, after the son of industrialist Carl F. Stage, who commissioned its construction. Cadets sail-trained on the ship in the Baltic and North seas. Australian Allan Villiers bought the ship in 1934, renamed it, and sailed it around the world. The Conrad eventually was turned over to the United States government, and in 1947 President Harry Truman signed it over to Mystic Seaport.

Margaret L. Pratt
Canon A2 - Auto

3

1

Ships big and small, short and tall, call
Mystic Seaport home. A short distance
from the Morgan (*far left*) and the Conrad stands the Seaport Light.

Laura Kahler
Canon AE1, Mystic
Color Lab 200, f/8

2

Mystic Seaport during the filming of the
movie *Amistad.*

Frank Rochette
Minolta, Kodak Gold

2

1

2

1

The *Charles W. Morgan* whaling ship at Chubb's Wharf at Mystic Seaport.

Len Wickens

2

The masts of the *Charles W. Morgan*, the world's only remaining wooden whaling ship, loom above the dusty streets of Mystic Seaport. Built in New Bedford, Massachusetts, in 1841, and named for its original owner, the Morgan sailed for eight decades, mostly in the Pacific Ocean, harvesting whale oil for use in lanterns and lubricants. In the 1840s she was just one of 600 whalers cruising the high seas, but the fleet dwindled after petroleum was discovered in 1859. The Morgan retired to her homeport in New Bedford in 1921. The 1938 Hurricane wracked the old ship, but it was brought to Mystic Seaport in 1941 and eventually restored. The ship is a National Historic Landmark.

Len Wickens
Ricoh ASA 100

1

2

1

Visitors at Mystic Seaport can delve into the full experience of life in a 19th-century seaside New England village. This horse-drawn carriage rolls past the Joseph Conrad.

Len Wickens
Ricoh ASA 100

2

In the days before electricity, printing presses were run by hand—or by foot, as with the one beneath the clock in this Mystic Seaport print shop.

Lynda Hodgins
Canon Rebel 2000 / EOS 300,
Kodak Max 400, f/22

3

Whaleboats are stored for the winter behind the Charles Mallory Sail Loft at Mystic Seaport. In the spring, they may again grace the decks of the Morgan or other ships. Mallory arrived in Mystic in 1816 with only $1.25 to his name. He died in 1882 the wealthiest man in Mystic after a successful career in sailmaking and later as an investor in shipbuilding and whaling.

Katherine Preece
Olympus OM1, 50mm lens,
Kodacolor Gold 200, f/8, 1/125

3

1

1

The Amos Williams house, circa 1807, is located across Main Street from Old Mystic General Store. Originally known as the Wayside Inn, it served for years as a stagecoach stop. Daniel Webster is said to have stopped for drinks on his way to catch a ferry in Groton in 1840.

Rowena Melville-Young

2

Theories abound about the "old stone house," a curious local landmark atop Quoketaug Hill in Old Mystic, along the Pequot Trail. Built in 1825 by Elias Brown, the first president of the Mystic Bank, the mansion burned down in 1924 when a servant mistakenly placed oily rags in a fireplace. Its stone shell survived the disaster intact, but the 1929 stock market crash postponed the family's plans to rebuild it. In the years since, it has teased the imagination of countless passersby.

Rowena Melville-Young

3

Lined up outside the Seaport's 1833 Mystic Bank building, these casks belong to the cooper's shop next door. Tightly crafted casks could carry whale oil, honey, whiskey, gunpowder, or any number of substances useful at sea or on shore. Their bulged shape offer several advantages; the metal hoops can slide up or down, for example, as the wooden slabs shrink or expand. Coopers often etched Roman numerals into each slab so that a cask could be put together in the exact same sequence if it were ever taken apart, thus assuring the tightest possible fit.

Carolyn Bearce
Sears SLR 35mm,
Kodak Gold 200, f/8

2
3

1

1

The charming Mystic train station will soon witness another historic event in American rail travel. Amtrak's high-speed Acela trains are scheduled to begin buzzing through Mystic in 2000. Local residents have battled rail officials in recent years over the loud whistles that trains must blast at crossings. Ironically, when the first tracks were laid through Mystic in the mid-1800s, residents petitioned the government to build them through downtown rather than across Masons Island to the south, as originally planned. The monument at the Mystic station contains the bell from the New York, New Haven, and Hartford Co.'s Locomotive 3249, which ran on the line between 1918 and 1946.

Rowena Melville-Young

2

Indian and Colonial Research Center opened on Main Street in Old Mystic in 1965, with the pledge to preserve the papers of Eva L. Butler, a respected local historian. Built in 1856, the building formerly housed the Mystic National Bank. It was sold to the Town of Stonington in 1889 and used as a voting hall as well.

Rowena Melville-Young

2

1

1

The Old Mystic Methodist Church on Main Street is a picture of Greek revival beauty.

Rowena Melville-Young

2

The B.F. Clyde Cider Mill in Old Mystic is the oldest steam-powered cider mill in the country. Six generations of Clydes have made cider here since 1881. The sweet stuff is pressed fresh daily from late September through December. A National Historic Landmark, the mill offers demonstrations each weekend. Visitors also can purchase hard ciders, apple wines, jellies, and fudge.

Rowena Melville-Young

3

This peculiar house on the Whitehall Avenue portion of Route 27 in Old Mystic was home to music teacher Simeon Gallup. A soldier in the Civil War, Gallup built the house around 1883. His descendants still own it. The Gallup family was one of the first to settle Mystic and the Whitehall area.

Rowena Melville-Young

1

2

3

1

Nathan Whiting (father to Hallam) built this house on North Stonington Road around 1810. It sits across the street from the Clyde family's cider mill. Whiting was a sieve-maker, as were all three of his sons.

Rowena Melville-Young

2

The Old Mystic Methodist Church.

Jeff Feldmann
Sensia 100, N90S,
35-135mm, f/5.6

3

Built in 1889 in the Fishtown section of Mystic, the Fishtown Chapel never had its own pastor. Local ministers took turns hosting worship services there, and residents also used the chapel for Sunday school. After years of neglect, the chapel was moved to Mystic Seaport in 1949 and now stands near the Spouter Tavern.

Joel Peterson

1

1

Winter has arrived on Cow Hill in Old Mystic, where this small barn tries its best to keep warm under a blanket of snow.

Wanda Boucher
Canon Sure shot,
Kodak 35mm, 400 speed

2

Bedecked with a simple wreath and a touch of snow, a roadside barn in Ledyard is dressed handsomely for the holidays. Incorporated in 1836, Ledyard is located immediately north of Mystic. The town was named for Col. William Ledyard, the commander of the American revolutionary forces at the Battle of Groton Heights in 1781.

Bernard Bartick
Minolta 3ki

2

1

1

The Chapman family's Riverhead farm
on Shewville Road is located in Old
Mystic. As Mystic's first settlement, Old
Mystic sprung up around the northern
end of the Mystic River and was there-
fore known originally as the Head of the
River. Whitford Brook flows into the
river near the farm.

Richard Ely
Nikon FM

2

Company arrives for dinner at a sheep
farm in Mystic. The rocky fields here
overlook a cove between Masons Island
and Latimer Point.

Mary Blanchet
Nikon 8008

3

Built in 1841, this house on North Stonington Road belonged to Hallam Whiting, an Old Mystic sieve maker house. It
remained in his family until 1935.

Rowena Melville-Young

1
—
2

1

Autumn's most popular crop, pumpkins sit outside B.F. Clyde Cider Mill in Old Mystic. Several local farms offer pick-your-own pumpkins each autumn.

Stephen Sisk
Nikon 8008, Tamron 28-200
zoom, Kodak Gold 100, f/11

2

An autumn canopy conceals only some of the beauty of the George Greenman House, part of the Mystic Seaport Museum. The Greenmanville Avenue section of Route 27 is named for the famous shipbuilding family. Brothers George, Clark, and Thomas Greenman established their first shipyard at the Head of the River—modern-day Old Mystic—in 1827. In 1838 they began building ships on what is now the site of Mystic Seaport. Over the next half-century they crafted 94 clippers, steamers, and other ships, including some of the largest of their time.

Stephen Sisk
Nikon 8008, Tamron 28-200
zoom, Kodak Gold 100, f/11

3

1

Young lovers often pause at the duck pond in Olde Mistick Village, a cluster of 60 shops in the style of an 18th-century New England village. A wishing well, an Anglican meetinghouse available for weddings, and the annual holiday Festival of Lights make the village an especially romantic setting.

Lisa Mendillo
Olympus 35-70mm 1:3.5–6.7

2

A model of Victorian architecture, the rust-brick Mystic & Noank Library in downtown Mystic was a gift from Capt. Elihu Spicer Jr. on Noank in 1893. An inscription above a fireplace upstairs in the library remembers Spicer so: "Large was his bounty, and his soul sincere." Today the library is home to Emily the Cat. Friendly but often aloof, Emily is a celebrity of sorts in Mystic. She was recently featured in a video about library cats from across the country.

John Williams
Nikon N70, Kodak
Gold 100 f/8, 1/125

3

The old gristmill at the B.F. Clyde Cider Mill hearkens back to the days when families ground their own johnny-cake meal. The Clyde family still does. They also make pies and pumpkin bread each fall.

Rowena Melville-Young
PO Box 248
N. Stonington, CT 06359

1

1

The Morgan as seen from the Conrad.

Joel Peterson

2

The little whaleboats suspended above
the decks of great whaleships such as the
Morgan played a critical role on whaling
journeys. When a crew sighted a whale,
several members would take to the
water in whaleboats to chase and har-
poon the target.

Joel Peterson

2

1

2

3

1

Seven thousand pounds of British Bower anchor stand in the yard outside Mystic Seaport's galleries. Found off Newport, Rhode Island, the anchor probably belonged to one of the British gun ships that blockaded the city during the American Revolution. Its wooden stock was reproduced at the Seaport.

Joel Peterson

2

A captain's wheel gazes longingly at the Morgan, perhaps imagining—or remembering what it feels like to be at sea.

Joel Peterson

3

The sun suggests patching the hull of this boat at Mystic Seaport's preservation shipyard.

Noank
and
Fishers Island

Noank, a peninsula with Morgan Point on the tip and the Mystic River on the west side, is very popular with sailors with the protected waters of Fishers Island Sound and the close proximity to Block Island.

3

1

Simmons' Castle guards the rocky shore at the eastern end of Fishers Island. The strikingly blue waters of the sound are its moat. Built of stone quarried in nearby Stonington, the castle is said to host a haunt or two.

John Williams
Nikon N70 Fuji
100 f/11, 1/250

2

Battered but buoyed: Ford's Lobsters shack in Noank has soaked up the sun and salty air of the Mystic River for decades. In the same village can be found the renowned restaurants Abbott's Lobster in the Rough and Costello's Clam Company.

Richard D. Dixon

3

The Latimer Reef Light off Stonington adds a splash of color to Fishers Island Sound. Built in 1884, it marks the trend toward iron lighthouses in the late 19th century. The light stands 49 feet tall and is equipped with a horn.

Beth Mulloy
Nikon N70, ASA 100

1

1

Boats rest on the pewter surface of the
waters near Morgan Point on an evening
in early autumn.

Paula Thomas
Asahi Pentax Spotmatic, Vivitar
auto Telephoto 135mm lens

2

The imperfections of a homemade pier,
one of many along the shores of the
lower Mystic River, makes Noank seem
only that much more perfect.

Richard D. Dixon

2

1

The masts of sailboats moored off Noank, and the Latimer Reef Light about four miles away, punctuate the silvery waters of Fishers Island Sound.

William Grant

2

The first Morgan Point Light was built in 1831 on land purchased from the descendants of James Morgan, one of Noank's first European settlers. In 1868 the lighthouse was rebuilt from granite blocks, in the same style as several other government lights of the era. Before it was deactivated in 1922 and removed, the light at the top of the 52-foot tower boasted a range of 12 miles.

John Williams
Nikon N70, Kodak
Gold 100 f/8, 1/250

1

1

For Noankers, sailing is in their blood, and to some it becomes an obsession at an early age. This young man looks for the starting line—and for another chance to conquer the waters of Fishers Island Sound—at the Ram Island Yacht Club's dinghy regatta.

Charles Wenderoth
Nikon N60, 28-200mm
Quantaray, Fujicolor Super HGII20

2

Gliding past the Morgan Point Light, a Blue J heads for home, eager to let the wind out of her sails.

Charles Wenderoth
Nikon N60, 28-200mm
Quantaray, Fujicolor Super HGII20

2

1

1

Wind and water and white sails collide
each October at the Race Rock Regatta
in Fishers Island Sound.

Richard D. Dixon

2

The Race Rock Light is a Gothic
Revival, granite masterpiece built under
precarious circumstances just off Fishers
Island, New York, in 1878. Several ships
had wrecked upon the Race Rock before
Francis Hopkinson Smith and Capt.
Thomas Albertson Scott devised a plan
and secured the necessary funds to build
the lighthouse. The project required
more than seven years and $278,000 to
complete. Some work was done underwater, and tons of material were needed
to build up the foundation and then the
light itself to a height of 67 feet.

Beth Mulloy
Nikon N70, ASA 100

96 THE MYSTIC COAST

2

1

2

1

The Sandra-Michelle is soggy from a
foggy day in Noank.

Teagan McMahon
Pentax K1000, Kodacolor 200, f/8, 1/60

2

A seagull steals the spotlight from the
sunrise in Noank.

Richard D. Dixon

3

The sunset drops anchor beside a yacht
at Noank. Across southeastern Connecticut, sunset lovers can find one quiet
cove after another in which to watch the
last brightness of day fade into night.

Linda Rambow
Olympus, Mystic
Prestige film

3

GROTON AND NEW LONDON

The Thames River, which forms the border here between Groton and New London, runs all the way from the inland town of Norwich into Long Island Sound. The river and its tributaries provided power to many of the mills that historically fueled the region's economy. Ironically, one of Norwich's own would turn traitor during the American Revolution and help lead the British assault on New London and Groton. He is Benedict Arnold.

Groton's Avery Point is home to a branch of the University of Connecticut and its marine research center. The Avery Point Light, built in 1944, was the last lighthouse built in Connecticut.

Points of interest in the New London area include the United States Coast Guard Academy, the Electric Boat Company—manufacturers of nuclear submarines—and the residence of Eugene O'Neil, as well as many other historic sites.

1

2

1

In autumn, Bluff Point—and so much
of Groton—becomes a kaleidoscope
of color.

Frank Kaczmarek
Pentax 645, 45mm lens,
Fuji Velvia

2

The sunset at Avery Point has stolen all
the color from everything around it. The
clouds and even the rocky shore are
reduced to dust at dusk. The Ledge
Light is nothing more than a silhouette
afloat in New London Harbor.

Lauren Rader
Minolta 430si

1

2

1

Milkweed and Black-eyed Susans take in
the fresh air at Haley Farm in Groton.
Designated a state park in 1970, the
198-acre farm contains some of the
area's most popular bike trails. Located
between Bluff Point and Noank, the park
is maintained today by the Groton Open
Space Association.

Frank Kaczmarek
Pentax 645, 45mm lens,
Fuji Velvia, f/22, 1/15

2

The spicebush swallowtail butterfly, one
of countless species that call Bluff Point
and rural southeastern Connecticut their
home.

Frank Kaczmarek
Pentax 645, 120mm lens,
Fuji Velvia, f/11, 1/8

3

Cinnamon ferns make a colorful under-
growth in the woods at Bluff Point.

Frank Kaczmarek
Nikon FM2, 35-70mm lens,
Fuji Velvia, f/22, 1/2

3

1

1

A dragonfly at rest in Bluff Point is but a shadow of himself.

Frank Kaczmarek
Nikon FM2, 90mm macro lens,
Fuji Velvia f/16, 1/2

2

The colors of autumn look twice as nice when reflected in the waters along the Bluff Point Coastal Reserve in Groton, established in 1963 as a state park. Depending on the season, the park is a favorite spot for hikers and mountain bikers, for shell fishers and cross-country skiers—not to mention abundant wildlife.

Frank Kaczmarek
Pentax 645, 200mm lens,
Fuji Velvia, f/22, 1/30

2

Autumn admires itself in this pond at
the Connecticut College Arboretum
in New London. The 435-acre park
contains hiking trails, thick woods,
and garden landscapes, and is a popular
destination for nature lovers and young
lovers alike. Connecticut College has
been ranked among the top liberal arts
schools in the country.

Frank Kaczmarek
Pentax 645, 200mm lens,
Fuji Velvia, f/32, 1sec

1

1

Grass seems to spring forth from the early-morning sky at the Bluff Point Coastal Reserve in Groton.

Frank Kaczmarek
Pentax 645, 200mm lens,
Fuji Velvia

2

Autumn dips its toes into the waters off Bluff Point in Groton. Mumford Cove to the east, the Poquonnock River to the west, and Fishers Island Sound to the south bound the peninsula.

Frank Kaczmarek
Nikon FM2, 80-200mm lens,
Fuji Velvia, f/16, 1/8

2

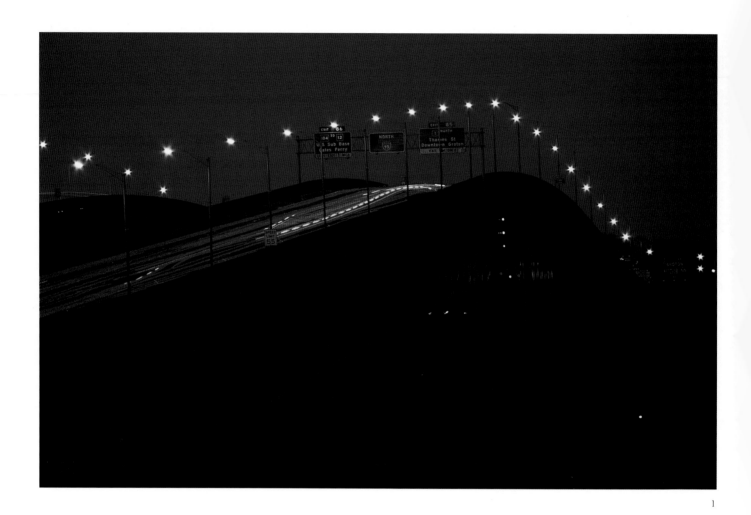

1

1

The Gold Star Memorial Bridge is ablaze
with the lights of motorists speeding
across the Thames River. The north-
bound span of the Interstate 95 crossing
was built in 1943; the southbound span
opened 30 years later.

Frank Kaczmarek
Konica FT-1, Kodachrome 64,
135mm, f/8, 2min

2

The lights from busy offices at Pfizer
Inc. in Groton reflect on the Thames like
giant candle flames. The world's leading
drug manufacturer came to Groton in
1946 as Charles Pfizer and Co. and established a plant on the site of Electric Boat's
World War II shipbuilding "Victory Yard."
Long respected as a vital employer in
southeastern Connecticut, the company
has earned worldwide acclaim through
the drugs it has produced—most notably
and most recently, Viagra.

Frank Kaczmarek
Konica FT-1, Kodachrome 64,
24mm, 2 min

2

1
—
2

1

The Nathan Hale Schoolhouse is named for one of Connecticut's most famous patriots. In 1776, the British in New York City hanged Hale without a trial for spying. Just 21 at the time, he was reported to have said at his hanging, "I only regret that I have but one life to lose for my country." Hale had taught in New London before his service in the war. The schoolhouse has been moved several times over the years, but today stands on Union Plaza.

2

Simple but strikingly attractive architecture lines Starr Street in New London. The Whaling City contains remarkable examples of conservative colonial styles as well as extravagant Victorian designs.

Betsy Hickey
Minolta Maxxum Htsi Plus
Automatic, Kodak 400

1

1

Triathletes of the future leave their bicycles strewn about the sunny sidewalks at Groton Long Point's South Beach as they prepare for an afternoon of swimming lessons.

Barry Thorp
Kodak Gold 200, f/11, 1/125

2

On a windless day these boats aren't going anywhere. They settle instead for another day at the beach on Groton Long Point's lagoon.

Barry Thorp
Kodak Gold 200, f/11, 1/60

3

Some sail in Long Island Sound. Others sail above it.

Margaret L. Pratt
Canon A2 - Auto

1

1

The USS Nautilus, the world's first
nuclear-powered submarine, was built at
Electric Boat in Groton and launched on
January 21, 1954. It remains today in the
Thames River, as a museum. Visitors can
experience the cramped quarters and the
thrilling responsibilities of the men who
served their country underwater. The
Nautilus was also the first ship to go to
the North Pole and the first submarine
to reach a depth of 20,000 leagues under
the sea.

2

The USS Providence slips past the New
London Ledge Light and out of the
Thames River one July morning. The
submarine is home ported at the U.S.
Naval Submarine Base on the Groton
shore of the Thames.

Peter Rodgers
Pentax K1000, Kodak
400, f/8, 1/500

2

1

1

The New London Harbor Light was one of the only four lighthouses standing along colonial America's coasts following its creation in 1760. Although the New London Harbor Light was able to withstand the Revolutionary War, it could not survive the effects of wind and weather.

Beth Mulloy
Nikon N70 ASA 100

2

The New London Harbor Light was rebuilt in 1801 after developing a 10-foot crack that had opened its walls. Today its tower stretches 90 feet above the banks of the Thames River.

Jerry Sims
Pentax 645, Kodak
Vericolor 160

2

1

1

The New London County Courthouse
has sat at the top of State Street in
downtown New London since 1784. The
colonial- and Georgian-style structure
replaced the original New London courthouse, which was burned by the British
troops of Benedict Arnold in 1781.
When a proposal to replace the courthouse surfaced in 1906, The Day
newspaper of New London asked
astoundedly, "Shall New London Raze
Its Own Faneuil Hall?"

Bernard Bartick
Minolta 3ki

2

Built in 1909, the New London Ledge
Light is arguably southeastern Connecticut's most recognizable landmark—or
watermark. Looming 58 feet above the
waters of New London Harbor, the light
boasts a range of 17 miles. Some locals
insist that the colorful French Second
Empire structure, complete with a
Mansard roof, is haunted by the ghost of
a former keeper who jumped to his
death in 1936 after his wife left him for
a ferry captain from Block Island.

Beth Mulloy
Nikon N70, ASA 100

2

1

Electric Boat on the east shore of the Thames River (left here) launched a submarine every two weeks during the height of World War II and its shipbuilding days. In 1952 it was the founding division of General Dynamics Corp., and two years later it launches the world's first nuclear-powered submarine, the USS Nautilus. It has built ships now in Groton for an entire century. Across the river is New London. Its ferry terminals, from which visitors can travel to Block Island. Fishers Island, and Long Island, are located just south of I-95's Gold Star Memorial Bridge.

2

The barque *Eagle* serves as the training ship for the U.S. Coast Guard Academy. One of the nation's four military academies, founded in 1876, the academy has called New London home since 1910. The city donated 113 acres to the academy along the Thames River for a permanent campus in 1931. The 295-foot Eagle was built in Nazi Germany in 1936 and named the Horst Wessel. The United States seized the boat after World War II and brought it to the academy in 1946.

(*following page*)

One of New London's ferries heads down the Thames.

LIST OF CONTRIBUTORS

Bernard Bartick
379 Wyassup Road
N. Stonington, CT 06359
pp. 75, 122

Carolyn Bearce
Scituate, MA
p. 67

Mary Nigro Blanchet
Mystic, CT
p. 77

Wanda Boucher
Mystic, CT
p. 74

Bryce R. Breen
brbre@conncoll.edu
pp. 14, 39

Peter Breit
Mystic, CT
p. 44(2)

Viola Breit
Mystic, CT
pp. 31, 50

Thomas Carver
PO Box 93
Stonington, CT 06378
pp. 10, 20, 21, 42

Carol Cattanach
13 Russell Street
Mystic, CT 06355
pp. 34, 48

Marilyn Chittom
2804 Confederate Avenue
Tupelo, MS 38801
(662) 841-9175
p. 52

Marilyn C. Cruthers
27 Benedict Crossing
Norwich, CT 06360-6461
mwcc26@aol.com
p. 25, 45

Richard D. Dixon
Baptist Hill Road, Box 5
Old Mystic, CT 06372
(860) 536-9778
pp. 22(2), 47, 88, 91, 96, 98

Richard Ely
PO Box 329
W. Mystic, CT 06388
p. 76

Jeff Feldmann
139 Sidney Avenue
W. Hartford, CT 06110
Feldmann@mail.Hartford.edu
pp. 58(2), 72

Mary S. Georgetti
134 Old Evarts Lane
Mystic, CT 06355
(860) 536 2217
MSGetti@aol.com
p. 56

William Grant
Noank, CT 06340
(860) 536-2126
p. 92

Elizabeth Hall
62 Cove Road
Stonington, CT 06378
p. 35

Betsy Hickey
Mystic, CT 06355
Betz@aol.com
pp. 46, 51, 116

Lynda Hodgins
3305 Pearl Street Road
Batavia, NY 14020
mhodgins@iinc.com
pp. 38, 39, 64

Frank Kaczmarek
11 Vermont Drive
Oakdale, CT 06370
(860) 859-3578
Frank_S_Kaczmarek@groton.pfizer.com
pp. 102, 104(2)-108, 110-113

Laura Kahler
PO Box 565
Old Mystic, CT 06372
Lak@uconect.net
pp. 29, 30, 60

Cheryl Kraynak
PO Box 329
Mystic, CT 06355
(860) 536-2520
C_Kraynak@Yahoo.com
p. 40

Marion Krepcio
2 Alley Way
Stonington, CT 06378
(860) 535-2559
Ryden13@aol.com
p. 28

Michael Marusic
Connecticut
MarusicL@hotmail.com
p. 56

Teagan McMahon
13 Terrace Avenue
Noank, CT 06340
(860) 536-6862
p. 98

Rowena Melville-Young
PO Box 248
N. Stonington, CT 06359
pp. 16, 26, 66-70, 71(2), 72, 77, 81

Lisa Mendillo
Connecticut
P. 80

Beth Mulloy
17 Robinhood Drive
Gales Ferry, CT 06335
(860) 464-9421
bmulloy@aol.com
pp. 24, 89, 97, 120, 123

Margaret L. Pratt
1848 Doral Park Road, SE
Rio Rancho, NM 87124
MLZPratt@earthlink.net
pp. 32, 33, 59, 118

Joel Peterson
Woods Hole, MA
JPNautilus@aol.com
pp. 55, 73, 82, 83(2)

Katherine Preece
100 W. 57th St
New York, NY 10019
(212) 262-1374
kjpreece@aol.com
p. 65

Lauren Rader
Mystic, CT
RaderLM@hotmail.com
p. 103

Linda Rambow
Groton Long Point, CT 06355
lerambow@snet.net
p. 99

Pam Reed
PO Box 815
Wilbraham, MA 01095
p. 53

Lieutenant Peter Rodgers, USN
USS Providence (SSN719)
M965646@aol.com
p. 119

Frank Rochette
17 Coburn Avenue
Mystic, CT 06355
p. 61

Jerry Sims
Gales Ferry, CT
p. 121

Stephen Sisk
299 Mistuxet Ave
Stonington, CT 06378
Sisk98@aol.com
Cover, 6, 15-18, 20, 41, 78, 79

Paula Thomas
Vero Beach, FL
Panda969@juno.com
p. 90

Barry L. Thorp
1227 Flanders Road
Mystic, CT 06355
(860) 536-0912
barrythorp@aol.com
pp. 116, 117

Len Wickens
The Joy of Photography
PO Box 5422
Magnolia, MA 01930
pp. 62-64

John D. Williams
6 Gale Avenue
Rockport, MA 01966
JohnRita@shore.net
pp. 8, 14, 23, 27, 48, 49,
54(2), 57, 80, 88, 93

Charles Wenderoth
Box 129
W. Mystic, CT 06388
pp. 94, 95